POSSUM AND WATTLE

My Big Book of Australian Words

Bronwyn Bancroft

LITTLE HARE
www.littleharebooks.com

I would like to dedicate this book to two of my close friends.
Euphemia Bostock for her unique and powerful use of words
and Sally Morgan who taught me the meaning of words.

BRONWYN BANCROFT

Little Hare Books
8/21 Mary Street, Surry Hills
NSW 2010 AUSTRALIA

www.littleharebooks.com

Copyright © Bronwyn Bancroft 2008

First published 2008
First published in paperback 2010

National Library of Australia
Cataloguing-in-Publication entry

Bancroft, Bronwyn.
Possum and wattle : my big book of Australian words / Bronwyn Bancroft.
978 1 921541 67 4 (pbk.)
For pre-school age.
English language--Australia--Juvenile literature.
427.994

Designed by Bernadette Gethings
Additional design by Xou Creative (www.xou.com.au)
Produced by Pica Digital
Printed through Phoenix Offset
Printed in Shenzhen, Guangdong, China, October 2009

5 4 3 2 1

Before European people came to Australia, it is thought that there were around 250 different Aboriginal languages spoken across this continent. Aboriginal and Torres Strait Islander peoples are very proud of their languages. There are still many people today who speak their language and who are passing it on to their children and grandchildren. Some Aboriginal language words are now used by all Australians and have become part of our national speech. Some of the words in this book come from a number of different Aboriginal languages. The pictures that accompany them have been painted by Bronwyn Bancroft, a famous Bundjalung woman artist who is very proud to share her cultural heritage with you.

SALLY MORGAN

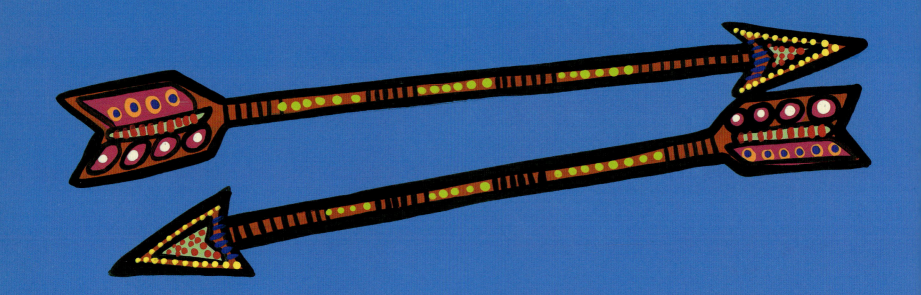

arrows

adze

apple

ant hill

ants

bat

bandicoot

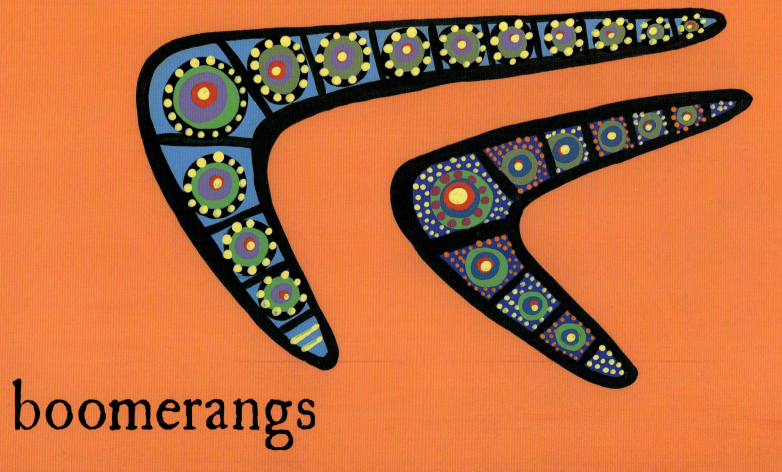

boomerangs

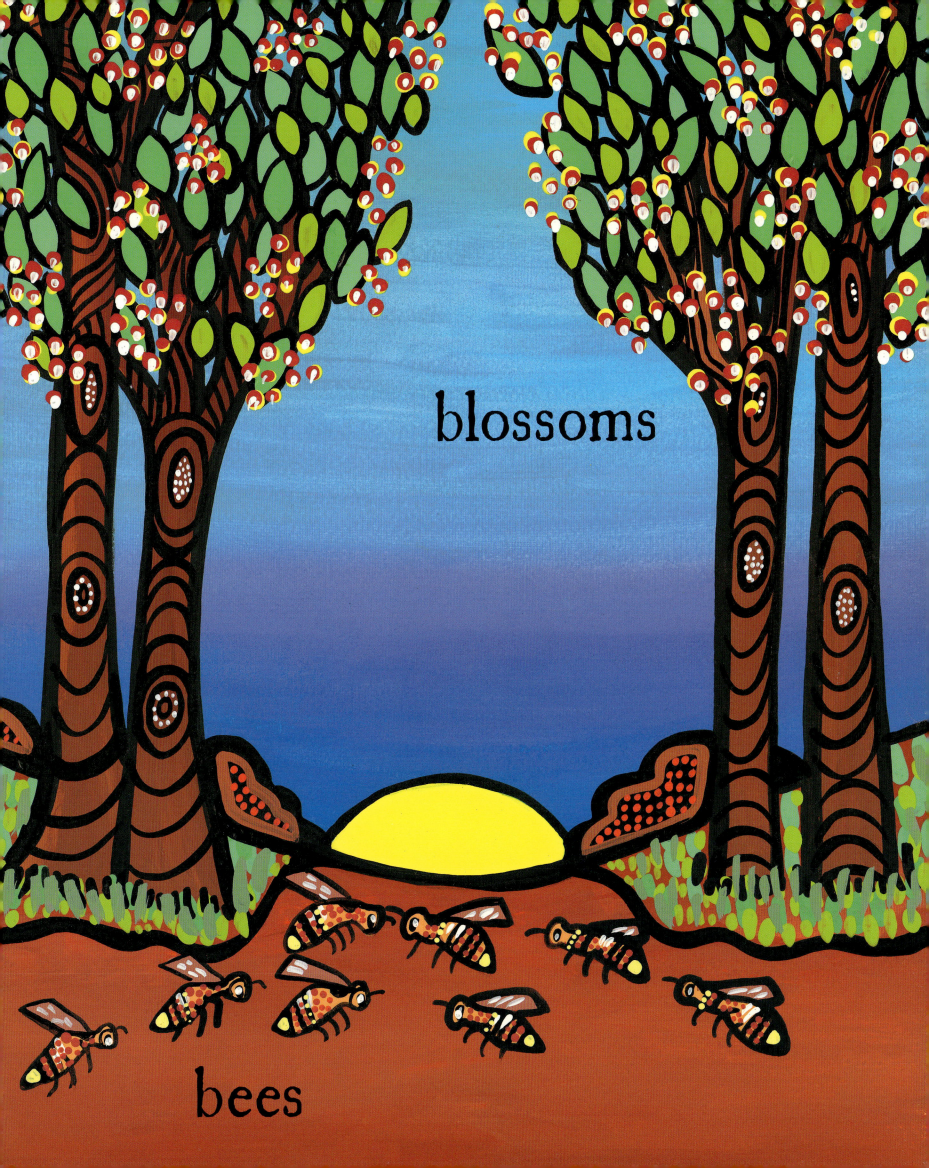

blossoms

bees

cloud

canoe

crocodile

cockatoos

dragonfly

didgeridoo

dingo

duck

dragon lizard

emu

emu chick

emu eggs

eagle

echidna

eel

flies

feather

frog

fish

flames

galah

gecko

goanna

gum trees

gumnuts

husk

honeycomb

hawk

hill

home

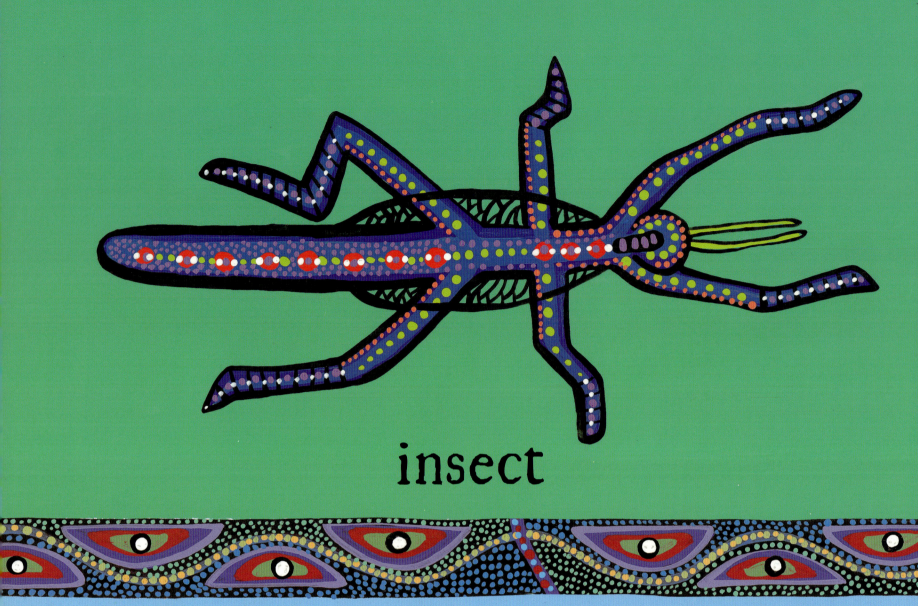

insect

island

joey

jellyfish

koala

kookaburra

kangaroos

leaf

lyrebird

lightning

lizards

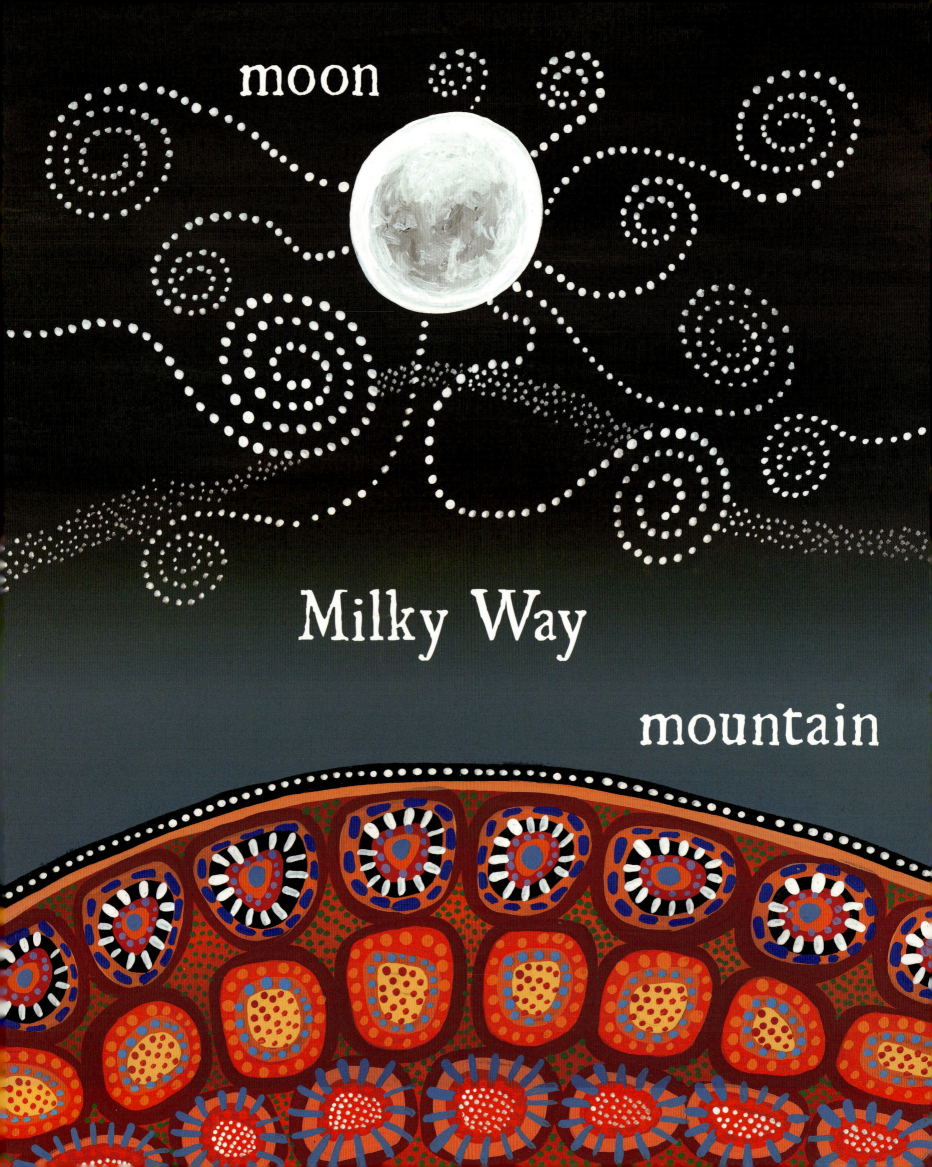

moon

Milky Way

mountain

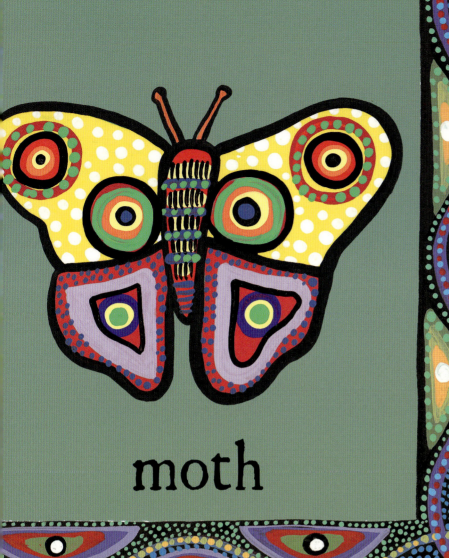

moth

mud crab

magpie

mushroom

nest

numbat

net

owl

opal

onion

octopus

platypus

porpoise

pufferfish

parakeet

possum

pelican

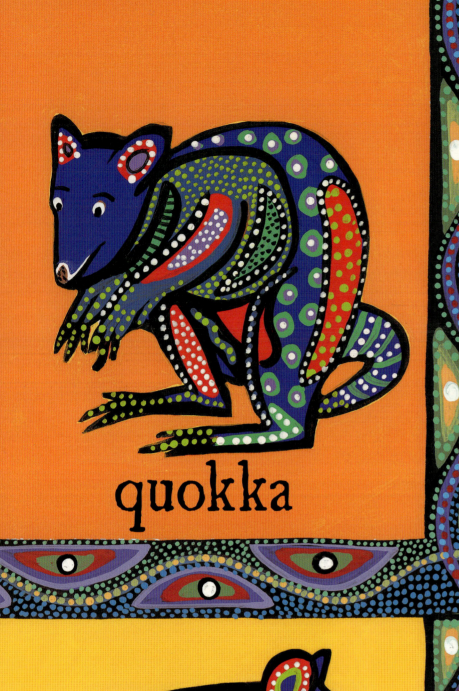

quokka

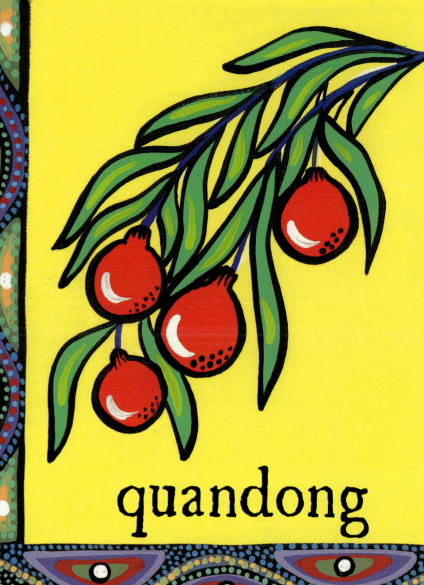

quandong

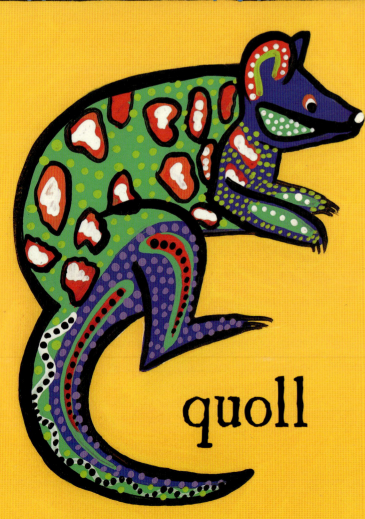

quoll

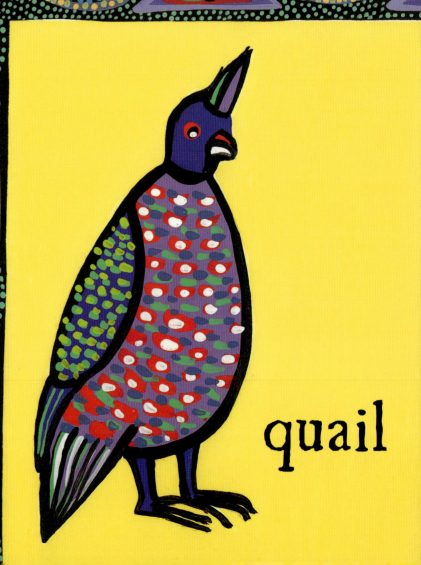

quail

rainbow

river

sun

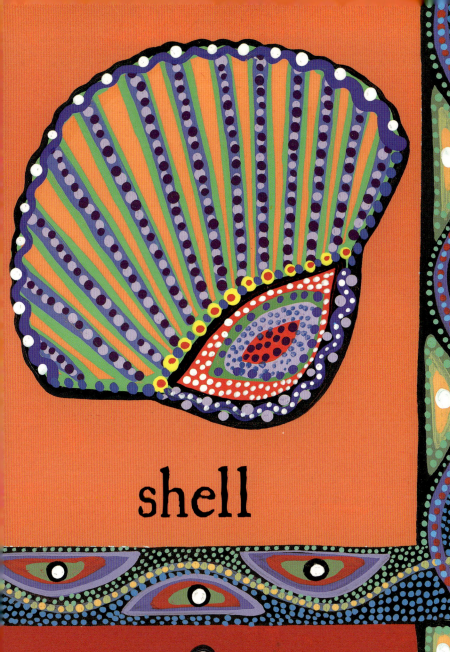

shell

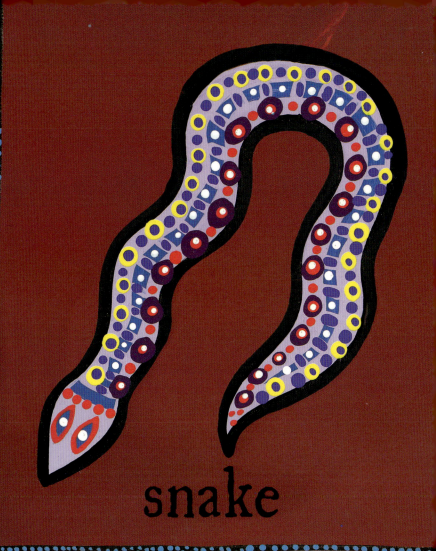

snake

snowflake

starfish

Tasmanian tiger

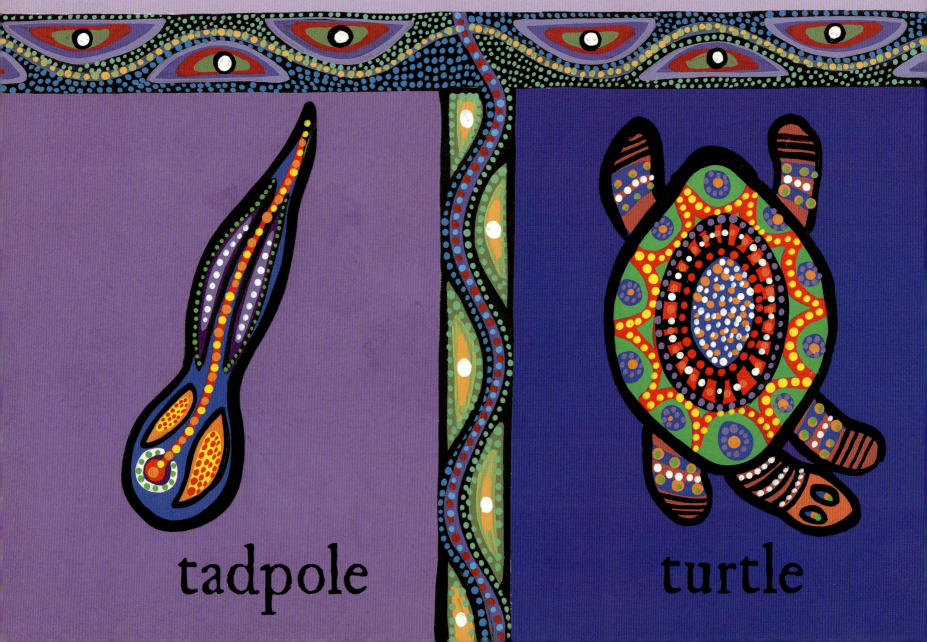

tadpole

turtle

tree

umbrella

unicorn fish

vine

vegetable

valley

wave

wobbegong

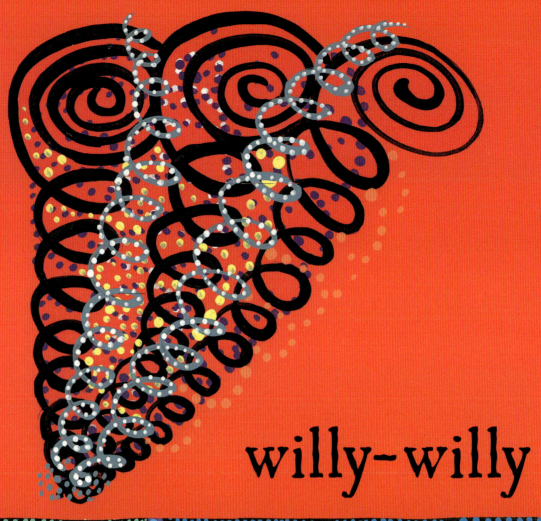

willy-willy

wombat

wattle

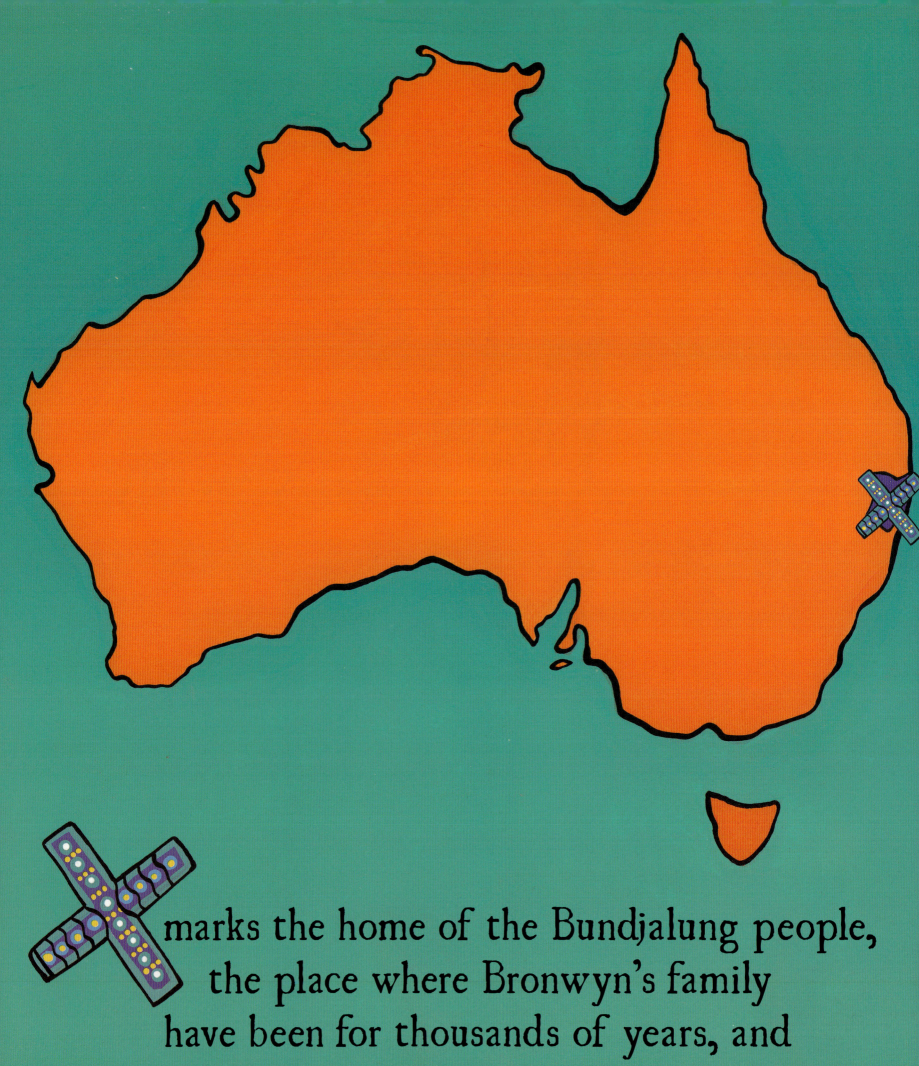

X marks the home of the Bundjalung people,
the place where Bronwyn's family
have been for thousands of years, and
where some of them still live.

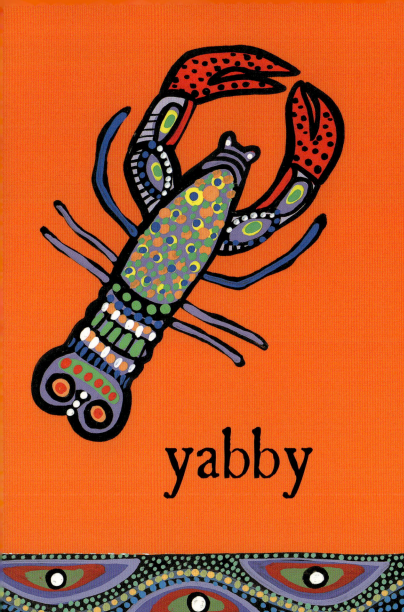

yabby

yam

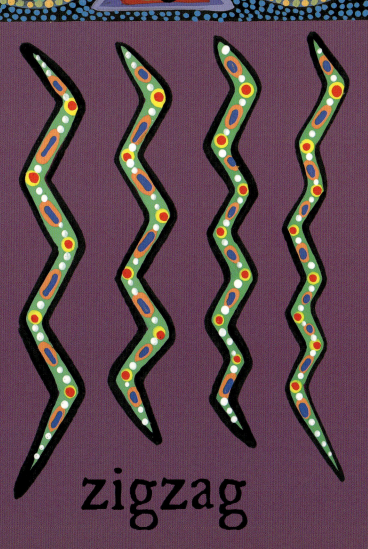

zigzag

zebra fish

SOME INTERESTING WORDS

Here are some of the words you have seen in this book. Some of the words are names for things found only in Australia. Other words are names for things that can be found in other parts of the world, but which have special Australian features. Not all the words in the book are found in the list below.

adze: a heavy tool made of stone and wood and used for working with timber

ant hill: a mound of earth built by a colony of ants, up to two metres high

ants: The honey ant keeps sweet edible honeydew in its swollen abdomen.

apple: The native Australian apple is known as a 'bush apple'.

arrows: sharp pointed weapons used for hunting food

bandicoot: small marsupials that look a bit like rats. They feed mainly at night.

bat: a nocturnal flying mammal. A common name for the fruit bat is 'flying fox'.

bee: There are over 1500 kinds of native bee in Australia.

boomerang: a curved piece of wood used as a missile. One type of boomerang can be thrown so it comes back to the thrower.

canoe: The bark canoe was one of the earliest types of canoe used by Aboriginal people in Australia.

cockatoo: a large, crested parrot. They are white, or white and yellow, or pink and grey, or black and red.

crocodile: a large thick-skinned reptile. There are both saltwater and freshwater crocodiles in Australia.

didgeridoo: a wind instrument consisting of a wooden pipe up to two metres long. It is possibly the world's oldest surviving musical instrument.

dingo: a yellow-brown Australian wild dog. Its call sounds like a howl or a yelp.

dragon lizard: a lizard with a frill, or beard, around its neck. They are also called frill-neck lizards.

duck: There are ten different species of native duck in Australia.

echidna: a small spine-covered mammal that lays eggs instead of giving birth to live young

emu: a large three-toed Australian bird that cannot fly. Baby emus are called emu chicks.

emu eggs: The emu-egg shell has many layers that range in colour from dark green to white. The male emu sits on the eggs until they hatch.

flames: Aboriginals have used fire to hunt, communicate with one another, for ceremonies and bush regeneration for thousands of years.

frog: Australia's smallest tree-frog species is able to catch a fly in mid-leap.

galah: a small cockatoo

gecko: a small lizard with sticky pads on its toes

goanna: various lizards that live all over mainland Australia

gumnuts: a woody inedible nut belonging to gum trees

gum trees: In Australia gum trees belong to the Eucalypt family. They are native to Australia, Papua New Guinea and neighbouring islands.

home: the shelter or dwelling place of a person, family or group of people

jellyfish: Jellyfish are not actually fish. They have a soft 'jelly'-like structure, with long trailing tentacles.

joey: the young of a kangaroo or possum

kangaroo: a marsupial with large hind legs for leaping and a sturdy tail for balance. Kangaroos have pouches where they keep their young.

koala: a tailless, grey, furry marsupial that lives in gum trees and eats gumleaves

kookaburra: a bird with a unique call that sounds like a person laughing

lyrebird: a ground-dwelling bird that has the ability to imitate sounds

magpie: a large black-and-white bird with a warbled song

Milky Way: the faint and distant stars that stretch across the sky at night. They can be seen spectacularly from outback Australia.

mountain: Mount Kosciuszko is Australia's highest mountain. It is 2228 metres high. The local Aboriginal name for this mountain is Targangil.

mud crab: a crab that lives in the mud of mangrove swamps

numbat: a small, slender, reddish-brown marsupial with a long bushy tail, a pointed snout and white stripes across its back

opal: a precious stone that is valued as an ornamental gem

parakeet: a small, slender, colourful parrot with a long pointed tail

pelican: a big web-footed bird with a large pouched bill that it uses to catch and store fish

platypus: A small furred animal with webbed feet and a duck bill, the platypus lays its eggs in a burrow with an underwater entrance.

porpoise: Similar to a dolphin, a porpoise has a blunt, rounded snout, is blackish on top and pale underneath.

possum: a tree-dwelling marsupial that ranges from the size of a mouse, to the cat-sized brush-tail possum

pufferfish: Also known as blowfish, pufferfish can quickly swallow huge amounts of water to puff themselves into a ball and stop predators eating them. Their spikes are poisonous.

quandong: a tree bearing bright red, edible fruit

quokka: a small wallaby found on Rottnest and Bald Islands off the coast of Western Australia

quoll: a cat-sized marsupial with white spots

snake: Australia has around one hundred kinds of poisonous snake.

snowflake: Yes, it does snow in Australia—mostly in the high country regions of New South Wales and Victoria.

sun: According to Aboriginal dreaming, the sun came out of the earth. The sun is central to the Aboriginal flag.

Tasmanian tiger: Also known as thylacine, the Tasmanian tiger is thought to be extinct. It was tan-coloured with black stripes.

tree: The boab tree (in Bronwyn's illustration) can be found in the Kimberley region of Western Australia. Some boab trees are over 1500 years old.

turtle: Of the seven marine turtles in the world, six are found in Australian waters.

umbrella: an Australian tree with large shiny leaves

unicorn fish: these fish live in outer reef areas from the south-west of Western Australia up to Australia's top end and then down to the central coast of New South Wales

wattle: a shrub or tree with clumps of yellow flowers

willy-willy: a spiralling wind of dust, like a small whirlwind

wobbegong: a type of shark with a flat body that lives on the bottom of the sea

wombat: a large marsupial with short legs and a stumpy tail that lives in big burrows

X marks Bundjalung: The illustrator of this book, Bronwyn Bancroft, is a descendant of the Bundjalung people of northern New South Wales and south-eastern Queensland. Her family still lives in the Bundjalung region.

yabby: an edible freshwater crayfish of central and eastern Australia

yam: a starchy tuberous root, usually of a vine

zebra fish: is endemic to Australian coastal waters and is found around most of Australia

ABOUT BRONWYN BANCROFT

Bronwyn Bancroft was born in Tenterfield, northern New South Wales.
Her father, Bill, was Bundjalung, Djanbun clan and her mother, Dorothy,
is of Scottish and Polish descent. As well as being a children's illustrator,
Bronwyn is a leading Australian artist and works in many different mediums.

Over her 30-year career, Bronwyn has participated in more than
200 exhibitions in Australia and overseas.

Her work is held in Australian collections at the National Gallery of
Australia, Macquarie University, the Art Gallery of New South Wales,
the Art Gallery of Western Australia and the Australian Museum. Her work
is also held in overseas collections including the Newark Museum, USA,
and the Volkerkunde Museum, Germany.

Bronwyn has illustrated several award-winning books for children.
Her most recent books with Little Hare have been the highly acclaimed
Malu Kangaroo (by Judith Morecroft), *An Australian 1,2,3 of Animals* and
An Australian abc of Animals. She received the May Gibbs Fellowship from
the Dromkeen Centre for Children's Literature in 2000.

Bronwyn writes:
Although I live and work in the city now, I know that my artistic
talent descends from my Old People—they have gifted it to me—
and I feel very honoured by that.